SALT:

the essential poetry of Lorette C. Luzajic

First Edition: 2021
Rs. 200/-

Cyberwit.net
HIG 45 Kaushambi Kunj, Kalindipuram
Allahabad - 211011 (U.P.) India
http://www.cyberwit.net
Tel: +(91) 9415091004
E-mail: info@cyberwit.net

Printed at Thomson Press India Limited.

Contents

The Ravine

My wish was carried inside of me,
silent as sleep,
to rest beside you
in an autumn ravine,
or spring, warm toasted
by the sun and close
to the earth.
I thought about merging
the last of our years,
last rites,
to find impossible ways,
ways we'd never found in our chaotic lives
of until, unless.
Imagine, what remains of our given days,
as one long riverbank afternoon,
tender madness?
What better way to herald pending doom
than to light a fire.
Let me offer myself,
perfectly imperfect.
Lie beside me, then,
before we are old.

Violet Hill

in the words of Van Gogh, remixed

I have two views
the gardens,
and the asylum

the walls are pale violet
the floor tiles red the chairs
fresh butter
yellow

still life:
majolica jug
with wild flowers

I am doing my best
I long to make
beautiful things

people will tell me
mountains are not like that
but in fact this expressed the remote, where there
are goat herds and sunflowers in bloom

I am sure they do not mean badly
they just don't understand at all and
probably think I am mad

Delacroix, you know he said
he discovered painting only when
he had no teeth left

the night café:
ruin madness crime
this dive of a bar

in death there is nothing sad
it happens
in broad daylight

there is no news
every day is the same

you must have noticed the sunflowers
I painted, they are in Gauguin's room
please, just let me get on with my work

I was thin and pale as a devil
working from morning to evening

I have been unable to stop myself
I could not let go
or take a rest

here is the stack of
orchards I had planned for you
impasto lilac and first white blossoms

white clouds in sunshine

blue enamel coffee pot
a cup on left, royal blue and gold
six different blues, five yellows

I went for a walk by the sea
along a deserted beach
how they sparkled bright green and yellow
white pink bright and still

opals, emeralds,
sapphires one might say
in the blue depths, these stars

it is not easy to paint yourself
it is different from a photograph
you are searching for something more profound
than what a photograph wants

I am always
laden like a hedgehog
sticks, easel, canvas, equipment, yellow straw hat
I am always dusty

believe me sometimes I have to laugh
at people who suspect me of all kinds of malice,
of absurdities I would not dream of

there is some sense
emerging in me of colour
something wide ranging and powerful

how I paint
I do not know myself

we are having very beautiful weather
chilly windy thunderstorms, rain

how good it is to walk along
the grey green sea
when you are feeling depressed
you have a need for something infinite,
something in which you can see God

my moods vary but I have acquired
a certain serenity
I have a strong belief in art
it is a powerful current

it carries man to a haven
but he has to put in an effort too

I will try to do
great compositions
the garbage dump with garbage men
people lifting potatoes in the dunes

the hands that hold the rope that rock the cradle

I would rather paint
the eyes of people than cathedrals
paint the soul of a human being
a poor beggar
or many beautiful women in the city

cobalt is a divine colour
so is emerald

it is no economy to deprive oneself
of these colours

when I get out I shall be able to get back to work
I shall start on the orchards in blossom again

the blue line of the alps
the peach trees the farmhouses
everything is small

if you can, see the olive trees right now
the foliage
old silver against the blue

just done two pictures of the asylum
a very long ward, with rows
the floor in red brick

a garden, a pond, very simple
and eight flowerbeds
Christmas roses with forget me nots

I can't help but dabble a bit
with my picture, same fields
ochre, violet under way or a moonrise

pink dahlias dotted with orange
and ultramarine:
wallpaper

but for the cypress tree
the pink sky
clumps of brambles

wherever the sun beats down:
this sulphur yellow

the violet hill

I saw all this like this
from between iron bars

it's too beautiful for me to paint it
or even imagine it

Gypsy Bisque

The warm soil scent of fresh tomatoes takes me to your funeral. It was late August, and my mother's garden was overflowing. Baseball tomatoes, perfectly round, heaped in bushels. Pancake tomatoes, broad and flat as fava beans. Lumpy tomatoes, splitting, spilling their pulpy seed stuffing, sewn back together by sun and rain.

You showed me how to make gypsy soup: it was nothing but flour and tomatoes, with a lot of paprika and a little bit of bacon or butter. You'll never go hungry, you said, stirring Serbia tenderly with a long wooden spoon. We added cashews, and cracked black pepper, poetic license.

If only I knew what I was getting myself into, I think sometimes, but I think I did. I knew I was in trouble the moment I sat at your table. You slid the tureen, the loaf, towards me, the wedge of fat for the bread, the small dish spilling caraway seeds. You looked at me straight on, then blew on the soup to tame its boil, but still I dove headlong into that burning ring of fire.

Crossing the River Jordan

After the lasagna
and some jazz and sherry
I tell them about the River Jordan.
How my father was hopeful, right up until
the moment we drove on. I wanted
to be dunked
at the source, in the same water
as Johnny Cash
and Jesus.
I had hoped
and hoped
to believe by the time I got there,
to join them in the rites of life and freedom.
I was the only one there who had
never been immersed.
In my heart, I thought
I would step down from the bus and
glide all white robed into the water, the creek
that is left of it, that I would confess
and profess, but then I didn't.
It was something I didn't take lightly,
so I stood back again. I could not just
profess something
for the sake of drama.
I did not go in.

Why not? Karen asked,
indignant with love.
You were there.

I tried to tell her that if I could not
confess with my lips,
I could not lie to God. It would
be blasphemy if I wasn't sure.
How sure do you have to be? Karen asked. At what
point is someone sure enough?
Even Mother Theresa was
sometimes an atheist.
Your own father hated God. The highest
priests, the most profound theologians, the apostles,
all of them were filled with doubt.

I had wanted to be drowned in purifying waters,
emerge magically new and whole on sacred shores,
all sorted out and certain. But Karen shook her head and
told me none of that would ever be or ever was.
How her own faith had
never been without struggle.
She asked again, How sure do you have to be? Hell,
Christ himself believed he'd been forsaken.

Karen had studied to be
a reverend. All that had been
left undone
was the official stuff,
but for some reason,
she didn't go on.
She had walked like me
to the edge of
that river, and then held back.

Gales Gas Bar

August will always
taste like hash and petroleum,
and it sounds like Guns 'n' Roses.
In those endless days,
the asphalt soaked up the sun
and spat it back out.

The gas station, it was the empire of my youth.
And it was a man's world then,
and that is why I loved it,
all pizza and Playboy,
guitar practice, Camels, Toronto Sun.
The farmers tipped me
with baskets of sticky peaches,
and I could spend my shifts flirting with
mullet boys in Mustangs and
mirrored sunglasses.

I watched how headlights
sluiced the falling darkness,
how night rose over the orchards,
how the concrete lot broke up the
vineyards on either side of forever.

And how the neon sign
kept blinking,
yellow, red,
alone for miles.
It was an Ed Hopper painting,
those gasoline summers,
tripped out on stars.

like a cat

making
love
to
you
is
so
purr

Walking the Dark

I can teach you the sound of trains
and how time shatters and restores
and you have taught me
what the heart can hide.

Mixed river heart-
how do I leave
that which has become
as bread and water?
When the blackbirds fly home,
I might be among them.

I have no obligation to tell you who I am
but I warned you what would become of us.
I said, do you remember?
I will be gone before I am gone.
How I am crashing, how the world is whirling
how my anxious arms are lead,
how the abyss, tacky and dismal,
has my future.
I told you I am dizzy and need help standing up,
how I'm tired of tragic tragedies,
of drama queens and picket lines.
How the sea reclaims its tears,
how freedom binds me in promises I can't believe.

these hands have touched the sea at either shore the dust and
the desert and the tar and the snow and the savage smile of
God they have hurt and helped and hitchhiked and they have

touched men and women saints and whores they have opened
doors and shut doors they have made bread and they have
made love but they have never made me happy

I cut myself on scorpions to find your heart.
You asked to look inside me
and I turned away.

I couldn't find you for the longest time.
Our distance was the darkest room.
Now you pace the roads as if they care cages.
How peculiar our borderlines!
The blanket that held your sleep so softly
knows only the brittle tapestry of bones.

For JL

don't be angry
at what I did
in youthful foolishness

I was terrified
of how much
I wanted you.

Motor City Agate

after *Reply to Red*, Yves Tanguy, 1943

"Scars have the strange power to remind us that our past is real." Cormac McCarthy

1. Once upon a time, your parties meant mopping our minds off the floor in the morning. Our bodies were shells by then, mere scarecrows. The relentless drum and bass went on until dawn cracked the new day open. At your latest party, you motion for us to keep things down while you put the baby to bed. I spend most of it in a corner, talking to a plumber.

2. Yeah, baby. We made it to middle age!

3. I was enjoying his company, truth be told. I liked how he talked about getting home to his wife, and to his job early the next day. I should always have had more respect for plumbers and electricians than I had for addicts and revolutionaries.

4. Your plumber friend had a strange kind of Bradburian beauty about him, overalls and all. All those worlds of submerged pipe mazes, nuts, bolts, twisting tunnels. The sheer efficacy of water works, the tumbling words about work that made him a poet at that party. He didn't mean it: he was like a deer in the headlights when I pointed out the way he found the phrases. He had never heard of Ray Bradbury.

5. Most of the party has absconded to your balcony to smoke. I have wistfully declined.

6. Flipping through a collection in one of your books on surrealist paintings, I see Yves Tanguy. It takes me away, to the moon, to Mars, to planets where books are banned and twine holds together the limbs of aluminium men.

7. His paintings remind me of Detroit Agate, those seamless coils of colour, winding ripples at once natural and industrial.

8. When my name was Raggedy, I lived in New Orleans in a burned-out plantation house with broken mirrors and the undead. At the local watering hole where we kept warm and drunk, there was a Deadhead chick with filthy feet and fingers and a gorgeous ring. I thought it was artificial agate, tie dyed stone, if you will. She said, no, this is Fordite. *Motor City agate*. Other rocks are millions of years old, she said. This one is only thirty. The swirls of purple and neon were made of paint trash from cars; harvested from the layers of melted slag that accumulated on the skids. Spray paint, other toxins, fused forever. The process for Detroit Agate was the same as every other rock in history, she explained, only with modern manufacturing speed. I wanted that ring badly. I covet it to this day.

9. My father worked in that same factory for forty years. Had a few years off between retiring and dying from renal tumours and their scattered seeds all over his insides. Forty years of whirring machines, midnights, suffocating temperatures, poisonous chemicals, long shifts. He said he loved his job.

10. That night, I was home by ten and sleeping soon after. I dreamed of my father in heaven. He was surrounded by rivulets of toxic enamels, the same sprays I use in my paintings. The seeping hues were changing to stone every which way he turned. He pushed his hands deep into the well, the melted mix of swirling colours, cupped them, raised them, told me, drink.

My Little Brother Shows Me Easter

There on the deck in the fading day of brittle spring
you let me see the moon
you held the telescope just so   and   then   just so·
and I might have given up looking for her-
I kept getting my eyes tangled in
trees, on the crackling grey paint on the side of a barn door.
I was shivering from cold

also from the spell of this great orange, rising, rising,
turning the billion-mile sky teal and finally,
shimmering hematite.
At the bottom of the sky,
the moon is almost red and then, at the top she is a transparent
frost,
the clearest, cleanest silver.   I cannot look away.

You are fixing and turning and adjusting
doing science and mechanical stuff with the tripod,
working in the few minutes left to catch this particular moon.

This moon only comes once a year, you say,
squinting into the telescope's gaze. It amazes me
how easily you unravel science, learn naturally the tools
with which to pry inside her.
You are gentle with her secrets,
asking simply, humbly to be led inside.
This reverence for God's creation astounds me.
Tonight, you are doing this for me,

to show me what I will never see in the city,
                    where you say I am walled.

I put my eye again up to the telescope,
expecting quivery branches in a blurry sky.
Instead   I see a serene fire
(the hollow mystery of craters).
Tears spring forth at this unexpected intimacy

at how close I felt to something actually out of this world.

(Earlier we were talking. We walked and walked and walked past fruit trees waiting on spring. We walked down to the creek and I wondered out loud to you how I could continue to live without listening to running water. It was a greyish creek with a few special features, but sometimes all you really need is water and a few trees. I point out how some plastic bags had blown here, how they are now stuck eerily like hanged men to branches of a naked tree. You look out through the orchards beyond the creek, on top of the wind in the plastic like flags. You look right through them and right through everything and tell me they are just corporate ghosts, blowing in the wind.)

The Limestone Angel

"I saw the angel in the marble, and carved, until I set him free." Is that Michelangelo's story of David, pale, proud puer, metamorphic masterpiece? This limestone angel, what was it like to sweep aside the stone and chisel him to life, tentatively, carefully, coaxing him to standing? Did the artist tremble at his touch, contouring calcaneus, mazza to mandible, scalpel to sinew, fingertips brushing across the tender loins of the boy who would be king?

The Broken World

Now that you have come
to sort things out,
I am more
confused than ever.
All hell
breaks loose
in midnight

and it's been years since
I heard midnight
knocking at my door-

I've made my life
so tidy
squished it crammed it stuffed it
with law and order.
I intended to keep
the crashing winds at bay,
as if lists and yoga, or sorted silverware,
could possibly protect me
from the gods of the sea.

I never know
if the roads
will bring you home, and
today
the miles
are written in your eyes,
the things you've seen,

the things you've tried to hide,
and you are wearing the sun
and the rain and the road
and the endless
prairie skies.

You are a storm that blows through here
galloping wild horses,
part human,
but something else,
something wilder, unrestrained.

It doesn't matter:
every time you
break my heart,
I will grow another one
for you to smash
and treasure the hours
in which
it falls apart,
just to have something from you.

I can't stop you
from climbing across my roof
and into my window
if you need to get to me.
Otherwise,
I don't even know if
you are dead or alive.
Now, the great unknown, again.
You disappear
as you arrive,
without words,

without reason.
Do you remember?
Once you said, you would do anything for me,
anything at all,
you'd walk 1000 miles for me, you said,
and the ferocity of your conviction took me aback,
how love blazed in your eyes,
for me.

It was a promise you kept,
arriving from the east
like rain on my roof.

But I had said, no, don't you remember?
I don't want it, I told you.
I won't ask that.
You know all I'll ever ask of you

is to put
your pipe down

for me.
Leave it down
I beg you,
leave it down.

I will never, ever
ask another thing.

Now as ever, your company is easy,
and holding you
is comfortable, familiar sorrow.
You ask about my work,

and about my meetings.
And whether I've found anyone.
My fingertips trail your scars,
fading rope at your throat,
feathers on your wrists.

Now, as if there were
no years between us,
and no grief,
we sprawl across the floor with
Johnny Cash on repeat, and it's
an apt soundtrack for all that we have seen,
for the people we have been.

And yours is a lonely road,
my most beloved friend,
but you've never questioned why I keep
your heart with me as best I can.
Even so, I told you.
It was how tenderly you tended to
my injuries, how you
tried to save me.

The air here is filmy and surreal,
emptied of you,
soapy and edged with grief.
I can't fix
the broken world.
It is you who could,
you who fixed my sink and my bicycle
when you hitchhiked into town.

It's only 2000 miles,
you said,
repacking your backpack.
I'm clean now, woman,
I'll make it west, don't worry.

Mezcal

I'd already decided I would try grasshoppers while I was there. If ever I would take such a leap, it would be to eat the real thing, in its context by people who knew how to make it delicious, not in those novelty insect eating kits I bought for my nephews and my brother on their birthdays. They could gnaw on stale scorpions if they wanted to, but if I was going to put a grub in my mouth, it had to come via someone's *abuelita,* someone who knew what they were doing.

We pass markets with green chorizo sausage and crates of tomatillos. Boars' heads split asunder and spread-eagled on ice. And mountains of dried peppers pile to the rafters, *anchos* and *guajillos.* Mole poblano, whole and powdered, as well as something else that you can't eat, to be sprinkled in the path, for hope, for good luck.

But no crickets or beetles, not yet. Just pretzels and puffy cheesies in bright green, fiery red, and classic orange. Here, they sell cigarettes by single. The lighter is tied to a clothesline, and you can tip a peso or two into a jar for using it.

We turn to the music. Something forlorn and moonlit, but there's a house beat underneath it. My friend has brought me to Zona Rosa- literally, Mexico City's Pink Zone. Two pretty young queens are necking on top of an old barrel. A little bowl of spicy beans lands in front of us. There's a table of five in the front window, heads thrown back to the night, laughing, free.

The waiter brings a tray of elegant little glasses, with limes and a bowl of crushed chili and salt.

This is worm salt, my friend explains, showing me how to lick my fingers. It is delicious.

You don't just swig it back like tequila, he says. Mezcal is more spiritual. You savour it. It's made from roasted maguey. He shows me how to pace the spicy salt, the lime, and the Mezcal sipping. It tastes like tequila but with depth and heat, like chipotle struck by lightning.

We take three rounds before getting up. The couple on the wooden barrel is still entwined, before twilight, in an almost empty bar. Something slides down inside of me, something melts, something light as a feather, heavy as loneliness.

In Memory

Why and wherefore, what and how
Does always discontent prevail?
Some tawdry tatters haunt the now
The scream, the sleep, how sweet the veil.
Create a summer, watch it fall
Delicious, messy, spun from dew
I'm freezing in this wintry hall
A severed hand apart from you.

Disappointment

I imagined Monet in his mist, shrouded by morning's last weight. Claude evaporating with the water, pushing pond lilies to the side of the pirogue with a tender oar, lifting the slimy pads to new light with a lover's hand. I'd read about his love affair with the lilies, felt flush thinking of the intimacy of his long looking. The caress of paint, in pursuit of pure beauty, how he dusted every water lily pad at dawn. It was an obsession against nature interfering with nature, recording truth that isn't truth, the artist taking her virginal, wiped clean, back to the start, again and again. The spell snapped like first love, shattered, upon learning about the maid. Claude hired a cleaning lady to tend to his passions, someone to dust and wipe his water flowers before he painted them. Another arrow through the heart of poetry. Well, then. Morning has broken.

The Dancer

shimmying shimmering
fishnets bursting stretched diamonds
for the fish in their constraint
slippery slow dancing
she makes me think of Josephine
with thighs as firm and plump
as eggplants

Play Doh

for Martin

Coffee with Noah, the last day of fall. He is learning to make kimchi, ever since he stopped making cider moonshine in his closet. We talk about our microbiomes, about eating more liver. We talk about carolling for Halloween and not Christmas, amused by the idea of warbling "Bela Lugosi is Dead" in front of retirement centres instead of "Joy to the World." Noah gives me a cell phone charm, a tiny Hello Kitty on a camel. It's something I have wanted for a long time. I wished I'd brought the little tub of plasticine from the dollar store that was at home on my desk. We could make blue spaghetti snakes, or little bunnies. We talk about how Cormac McCarthy should write short stories, even though he sees no point to them. The shorter the better, I think, argue for taking that lean language to its logical conclusion. Noah blinks both eyes behind his rimless glasses, considers Cormac flash, worries at a cube of sugar on the saucer with one pointy finger. He asks about Barcelona. I try to express a fraction of what it was like to see Gaudi's spires and all those legs of ham. Well, Noah always wanted to hop a freight train and hobo his way across the prairies and he tells me how he did, in June, from here to Medicine Hat. I picture him with his diary and a thermos of fermented cabbage tied in the very kerchief now on his head, soaring away in lonely locomotion. I imagine the slow stumbling stall as the train breaks in Alberta, spilling Noah and his notebook into the night, scattering a fluffle of hares.

Bad

bad boys
smoke dope wear sneakers and black leather
nowadays with pants that hang below crotch
level, and ugly hats

but bad men
slink in olive suits and gold watches
read beat junk on subways

bad girls
sit on buses, back seat window
with sunglasses and blackberry lips
bad women

write letters to killers in prison
and think
how close to death
they have never been

Jean and Suzanne

he can't draw,

and she's
afraid of
everything.
her lovers know the rules:
no guns
in the bedroom.

he says his paintings
are jazz.
he cries
over billie
holiday's
unmarked grave.

once upon a time,
a man
who can be counted among
the great loves of your life
told you about Jean and
you grumbled something
about overrated outcasts
(you were still too young to know
anything worth knowing
in those days)

this same man once
kissed you because

Tom Jones was singing
on a jukebox at the
Winchester Arms Hotel
(now a Starbucks)
kissed you like you never thought he'd kiss you
and never kissed you again,
no,
not like that,
and you never wanted him to
because it might take away
something from that night

it was this man, too,
who said your work reminded him
of Cy Twombly's.
there was no Google then; it was not until
later
that you read how only Cy
of any painters
was allowed
to make pencil scribbles
on his paintings.
ah, well, you did not know
and all your work has pencil scribblings
and it is too late to stop doing
exactly what you are going to do
to stop doing
exactly what you want
(and that is what this man who kissed you
with an audience of irate bikers
who did not like Tom Jones
at the Winchester Hotel
saw about you and loved.)

you do not recall the complete details
of all those afternoons
spent swaddled in the arms
of red wine.

but,
it is also true
that love
is brutal and lonely;
it means spouses, choices,
death and children

and
other
disappointments.

now you are almost forty
you still can't draw
but can't has never stopped you
not from anything but success, that is
you fill those canvases
you fill those pages,
the terrible law of averages
means obscurity for the great and for the small.
you accept that.
who will read your books?
you will still write them for those few, for
this man, the one who was always up
for another long story, long after
all
the others
had gone on

and now
he too
has gone on

and that is how
it goes-
those
who loved you
have turned
to ghosts

and how do you live a life
when all the living has gone out of it,
when everything you knew
has turned to dust?
you also miss the one
you married by mistake,
the one who changed you
the one who told you
to go and meet your fate
the one who gave you new eyes,
and then he gave you coins
to put over his.
now here you stand:
the whole earth is his grave.

but you live,
that is what you do,
it is what you can't help,
this hunger to create,
which you will do even if
no one is left to see it
or no one wants to
it is why you are here

but once upon a time,
oh the parties,
oh, you would not believe
oh, you would not believe
the music.
you could see in voodoo.
you were still up to see
the sunrise flooding the world with light
and you were still up to see it go down
and oh, the magic
of those potions and those powders
they caused the great and
the empires to crumble,
so you forgive yourself.
it was so beautiful at first
oh the music it was too much
how it could move over the beach and
out across the water how the
oh how the stars
would dance

and after,
way after,
after you had moved on,
the way you always will
to wrench every poem
out of every ordinary moment,
to paint, to live alone, working furiously
you showed some work,

they were
big white paintings
they were about clean

they showed your emptiness
to anyone who cared to look
and few did

but *some* did,
the man did,
he was there
he was always there,
even when he wasn't.
there in your aloneness
at the edge of
the end of
the world
there he stood
looking at those big white paintings,
those paintings about emptiness and clean,
looking into your devastation and sorrow
hand on his chin
searching them
his eyes far away
then he turned
and said

this is your best work yet, baby
you know that don't you?
as if I was a real artist or something.

You Took Me into the Woods

to see how autumn had just that day spun down to gold. It grew dark and your tongue felt like the same soft rain that fell before we got there. I left the ravine with bruised lips and straps to adjust, and somehow more innocent than I had ever been.

The Crayola Haikus

sunglow
sky blue
denim

scarlet
maroon
macaroni and cheese

orchid
goldenrod
yellow green

chestnut
dandelion
robin's egg

wild watermelon
tumbleweed
razzmatazz

lavender
gray
apricot

melon
copper
mango tango

electric lime
sea green
inchworm

cornflower
royal purple
wild blue yonder

Cloud Water

Just before he knew he was sick, my father took me to a dinner theatre in a barn to see the Christian Blackwood Brothers do Elvis. The roast beast was blander than British, and the horseradish ran out before I got to the line, but the gospel according to Elvis raised the rafters.

I'd never had a thing for this velvet-throated bird: his pout was pretty but I never was convinced by all those sequins and spangles. Just didn't feel his soul in all of that. Turned out, that was true, sort of. The pomade and the girls and the bright lights had their allure, but they say all the King really wanted to do was sing about the King. When he did, all that was missing came together. His heart in his voice. All night, just him and his band, when the hordes had gone home.

A woman in the powder room mirror at intermission was fixing her lobster-purple lipstick. She had Indian eyes but her hair was so pale you could see through it. She was talking to a friend in a cubicle that I could only see by some pointy toed boots peeping out and the jeans around her ankles. The disembodied voice from the toilet was saying something about Elvis, about how he once saw Stalin in the clouds, before the apparition turned into Jesus.

"And the good Lord said, Elvis, behold I come to you as living water," she was saying, and I could almost feel the rush of the rapture in the air with the flushing of the toilet. The sound was like a waterfall in Eden in the small stalled walls.

After my father closed his eyes for the last time, I came across the brochure for the barn show where we'd been. I pictured the bales of hay we rolled past on that blue and shiny day. The river tumbling under the clouds was a black ribbon between sky and earth, like the innards of a cassette tape slinging south through fields and branches. In my memory, I could hear Elvis lowing sweetly from those clouds, saw Daddy ascending through the pick-up truck to run towards him.

Petra, Jordan

It was the saddest horse, grey and weary, he could barely
hold me. I felt sorry, too, for the young man
who had taken the five dinar.
His mouth
was too full of teeth every which way,
even with some missing,
and his face was crooked and flattened and
hardened by the desert. He was
beautiful,
he had a wrangler-jeans kind
of swagger and
glittery obsidian eyes.

...

Some of the women wear
heavy kohl on their eyes and
a darling little girl
holds a baby goat.
One dinar, please, she says in perfect English
when I snap her picture.
On a towel, another little girl sells pebbles and scraps. Her father
is behind her, up a ways,
with a hammer,
chipping them out of
the desert wall.

...

On their last legs, the horses took us
the last leg of our journey,
delivering us from the stark city that had been
chiseled from rocks. We had walked for hours over
ancient bones and stood
in tombs and pagan temples,
under an ageless boiling sun.
For us tourists,
the weather was perfect, but
locals said it wouldn't rain
for six more months, at least, and that soon
it would reach 105 degrees.
I couldn't imagine this place, how it would be.
These blazing rose gold rocks,
the camels covered in colours,
and bells, an enchanted world,
and the Bedouin jewels, molten metal melted over open fires,
these blue and carmine gems,
metal trinkets stirred in the dark.

...

Inside the cool and secret shroud of the earth,
this cave, carved
millennia past to the Nabean goddesses,
then, a monastery, made by monks.
When I in awesome wonder
consider all
the worlds thy hands have made...
We have climbed
we are weary
but here, at the top, this temple.
we sing.

Then sings my soul
how great Thou art
how great Thou art...

Our voices are pure like bells inside these walls.
We are tired, and spellbound
solemn,
ragged with psalms.

Balconies

for Japey

I remember warmth
and think of being with you
late nights
balconies
under the city sky
we would just talk
and watch
the world go by.

The Sperm Trees

It was June, in Allen Gardens, at Sherbourne and Gerrard. Night was coming. Dogs frolicked in the fountains. I heard the sound of sirens, and everything smelled warm and fecund, like semen. The tiny pale petals of the Callery Pear had swept across the park, summer snow, spilling trimenthylamine, dimethylamine. The dusk was ripe with volatile amines, pungent perfume like yesterday's sex. I was already floating with the fireflies above those sperm trees, watching you tapping at my body with frantic fingers.

I don't think she's breathing, you cried to a Chinese T-girl who had stopped to ask you for a bump. I was only with it enough to know you nervously offered her a cigarette. I heard the small spark and inhaled a gravelly memory of nicotine. I felt her soft wrists and hard breasts against my face and arms. I smelled lavender and peppermint, piss and honey. Heard her say, *she is, but barely.* Someone's mobile phone clattered to the stones, someone scrambled for it, someone said into it, someone took too much of everything, who knows what. I was far away from all of you and from those gardens, somewhere lonely and tight like the closet I would where I would hide from mother's episodes when I was small. A place where all the noise and fear faded to white. I could feel the smooth nub of that worn green carpet on the soles of my small feet. I could hear the muffled, gleeful barking of the hounds running the park, but the twirling warning of the ambulance was louder, metallic and clear above it, like an oboe.

When I returned, I didn't know where I had been, or how long I'd been gone. You were all seated in a circle, inside, on my filthy floor. You asked me how I was, wanted to know what it was like, that remote place, that space where I'd gone where I couldn't feel anything at all. You wanted to know what they'd done to me in the hospital, and how I ended up back home. I didn't know what you were talking about, and I didn't want to talk about it. Wiped the rivulet seam of scum from the corner of my mouth, asked if someone could cut me another line.

I Am Not Afraid of Adjectives

or of adverbs,
I'll tell you that straight up,
just to clear the air.

paltry frisky spooky
glacial palatial

hackneyed tautological lush
resplendent renegade
wan

sagacious pedestrian opulent salient

spare glittering gaunt
sequential

auxiliary endowed caustic bellicose corpulent egregious

didactic
hubristic
jocular (LOVE this one)
recalcitrant (oh, it's good, it's so good)
rhadamanthine- (though I'll never use it in a sentence)

lothario (yes, a noun, but it shouldn't be)
tantamount wraithlike bromidic cowardly mundane
insatiate pertinacious vacant garrulous

I am, I am garrulous, yes,
and these are perfectly good words after all.

I do not want to be
another frugal and bitter Hemingway.

Sometimes density matters,
like Sharon Olds, all of her
stories stuffed with words spilling over.

And I'll raise you Ray. Bradbury
taught us to layer and stack
dizzying sentences,
gorgeous jumbles of
tumbling words.

Yes, yes, they say in every *Writer's Digest,*
every graduate and every undergraduate lit class and
every writing course, every interview
with every famous author-
only write the necessary words!
We must never have too many notes!
But I raise you Mozart, and declare,
I have only as many notes as I require.
If every excess was eliminated,
what will become of Dostoevsky,
or of the Psalms?

What of Murakami's signature shirking
of "show, don't tell"
for the eerie, wordy narratives that define him?
Will we still teach Yeats and Wilde?
Brevity is the source of wit,
only if and only if.
Yes, Orwell was terse and so he should be,
but surely Miller and Melville could use a red pen?

And Marquez? Only a fool would touch his
exalted, labyrinthine language,
but there are many fools.

The Beachcomber

for Pat Moffatt

Your rusty old van, not much life left in it. Us finding our way to the yard sales of the Beach rich. That's what Saturdays were for. On deck, old blues, or maybe Seger, maybe Steve Earle. Your flannel plaid shirts, your red and silver curls. A smattering of orange freckles under the eyes and on the back of your worn hands. An ever-lit cigarette, that grand moustache. You talked to me about Van Gogh, a hero no one guessed unless they knew you. It was all you wanted, as an artist: your life's work chasing that blue and yellow impasto and light. After hunting for vintage catalogues I could collage, for discarded paint-boxes for you to wrest back to life, we would find a bar as far away as we could get, towards the water treatment plant and the end of the line. Cold beer and suicide wings. I couldn't have known that you would soon jump, erase the space between the risen bluffs and the great lake below, but I had an inkling. You drank hard. Said the drinker in you had never left Thunder Bay. What could I say to you? The shit I'd downed was even harder. For all those trinkets that we found combing the Woodbine beaches, I don't have a thing from you. Sometimes you'd give me a kind of awkward fatherly pat on the shoulder and call me buddy. If I felt a kind of sadness there, at the very core of my being, I pushed it aside, brushed right by that inexplicable longing to write your name out in the sand.

The Marilyn Variations

this bitter earth
this milk and honey
come closer, take a sip

her hands, humble enough to learn
gefilte fish, chopped liver
from Mrs. Miller, as Mrs. Miller

look, how she is
covered in freckles
the kiss of the sun sprinkled under her eyes

the gleaming smile
genuine, at least as often as it wasn't.
I know how pure joy sometimes exists alongside utter darkness

her talismans-
her diamonds,
her pills.

where have you gone, Joe DiMaggio?
nowhere
I never left her side.

yards and yards
of crinoline
tiny, tired toes

the bluest water
Codachrome
the camera is home

Wikipedia:
James Dougherty was an American policeman
best known as the first husband of Marilyn Monroe

soft and sleek in red velvet
the vulnerable nipple
nothing so erotic as her books

apricot
parasols, Lucite heels
rhinestones, coral mouth

Jello jiggle
hello wiggle
how delicate the skin of her wrists

the daisy day:
how her photographer said,
it'll end in tears

sweaty thighs
slippery stockings
the moon circle of white calf.

miles and miles of lines
under her eyes, watch, says her director
how rarely she ever needs to use words

Arthur, forever maligned
for not seeing her
for not saving her

so many blame him
but he mourns her
even from his grave

the transcripts we should never have known
the saddest irony- a woman who launched a thousand ships
never got there on her own.

director: The Misfits:
She had no technique. It was all the truth.
It was only Marilyn.

Marilyn, golden
silver, covered in sequins
the infinite jest

no makeup
just champagne
and the sea

The Piano Man

The first time you visited him at the hospital, there was a gray, thin man who played at the piano. His hands were shaking, but his notes were pristine white flames. By chance you and your friend are talking about those years when you would see him like that, shuffling to the visitor station in ill-fitting jeans and fuzzy slippers. The memory brings the musician to mind, but your friend shakes his head when you ask if they stayed in touch. The piano player is gone, he tells you. Infuriated by the voices in the treble bridge, he'd hurled himself through that double paned window. Landed right on the doorstep of the shop where they made the toffee twist donuts you'd bring with black tea. You can still recall what the man sang. *I'm sure that I could be a movie star if I could get out of this place…* The ragged edge of him quietly burned a hole right through you. Sad, isn't it? your friend says, and you both know what the other is thinking- how easily it might have been one of you, instead, how hard you had both tried to abandon ship along the way. You think about the piano man on the psych ward at Mount Sinai, how he might not know that anyone had noticed his music, that anyone might notice him missing. Or maybe he did. It wouldn't be enough. You tell your friend you are bereft during the times that you lose touch with each other. Sometimes it's like that: you are seized with a small and sudden panic over circumstances you can't control. You think about the thin man, how he had already been a ghost. His heart of glass, that pale blue flare.

Yakshi

Yakshi, a two millennia old
fertility goddess. Of all the world's
great faiths, says Sister Wendy,
only Hinduism completely
understood the sacred nature
of the human body.
How here, Yakshi's arms and legs and
breasts, too, have all been broken,
eroded by time, and still.
Still, her beauty is humbling.
Yes. The cleft mound
between shattered thighs
is warm,
even as stone.

I admit, I approached her
with regrets. I was too lost,
too selfish,
for children.
I stood, as she stands,
before men, as a temple,
but also as a beggar,
down on my knees.

Men and women write, they paint,
they compose, about opening,
awakening, but what about
the closing of the body,
what about the shift of

the soul, when possibility
turns barren? We watch
helplessly, as our sex becomes slack,
as we spread from seductress into
flabby vestiges of purpose,
or gristle on dry bones.
Yakshi, I tell her, I used to turn heads,
and break hearts. Now,
my own palms
hardly seek me out,
how seldom does yearning
overtake me
from the practical matters at hand.

Daily Bread

It isn't that she's gone blind.
It's only that scarlet things
don't exist, in his mind.
Anyway, they aren't forever
she insists,
and draws, and turns out lists.
In the surplus of the weather
sifting through your wholesome grains
I feel like it is Sunday
and I feed on bread and rain.

The Photograph Not Taken

Pittsburgh, we weren't there an hour
and already I had taken a hundred
pictures, Carnegie facades and bridges,
a wonderland of texture in cement and steel.
But just ahead of me was
the best photograph, if I could get it,
a skinny boy, all gangly grace,
jaunty in green from
head to toe, green socks, green kicks,
green hat, green shorts slung so low.
He was whistling and carrying a hoagie.
The sandwich was almost as long as he was.
It was a moment of perfect, peculiar joy.
I fumbled for my camera.

But there was no picture.

Everything happened:
my camera clattered to the ground in a jumble of
flailing limbs, and the sandwich too, smashed
as some kind of sick jitterbug tore through him.
My heart stopped as he jerked in one terrible jolt,
propelled into the blasting wail of traffic.
Smack, the sound of his face hitting pavement,
more convulsions ripping through him without mercy.
His glasses broken, blood,
the bus about to pull away and
the boy under it.

We dived for him,
there was no
time to think, he was
heavy, we pulled with all our might, we
hollered for dear life, pounded on the side of
that bus. And oh, thank God, all of us, back
on the sidewalk.

His mother
would not know how he lay bleeding across
my thighs, cushioned from concrete,
waiting for an ambulance to come
as the seizure finished in my arms.
She would not know because
he would not tell her,
he would not remember, nothing but a snap of
electricity before blackness,
before waking to a
throbbing headache and confusion and
the relief of a nurse's warm hand,
outstretched with
a tiny paper cup filled with pills.

Later, J. and I, drained of adrenaline,
solemn with the magnitude of what had
happened, crouched in the corner of
a burger joint and nursed icy sodas.
J. noted wryly that it was good how things
turned out- she had not left her two young children orphaned.
And I observed the irony, of that old cliché:
would you throw yourself
in front of a bus for someone, and if so, who?
I would have said no, I said,

I noted a few exceptions, maybe,
maybe her, maybe my brother, maybe M. or J. but
they were already dead.

The city buzzed on as if nothing had happened.
Because nothing had happened, not really. People
were living and dying right there anyways, outside
of that little twist of fate. We walked all over,
watching the water from the yellow bridge, I was
in a kind of fuzzy daze, on some kind of tightrope.
On the edge of fate, of having changed it,
in some small way.
I could not wrap my head around the randomness.
What if we had gone to Boston instead? What if we
had walked slower, or browsed longer in the gallery?
What if I had not noticed the beautiful black boy,
and wanted to take a picture of someone else instead?
In that infinitesimal fraction of a second before
I would have snapped, a cataclysm. A world changing.
And nothing changing. Marko and Japey and
the rest of them, still dead.
But you don't get to choose
whose lives you save.

Damage

You pace along the drizzling streets of October,
and your thoughts are winding storms.

You can't be sure he is prepared for the life of a poet,
for the rain-soaked rooms your soul hides.

It has never been other men that your lovers have envied,
but intangible threats like orphans and the sea.

How now, love? after sealing yourself
from its seething gutters and radiant suns,
after shutting down the heart, even the body.
Live by experience
is already your epitaph.

You can't be certain, but you believe he sees how you see.
Still, you fear those less complicated,
shiny girls with firm handfuls of thigh, smooth and poreless
breasts that rise effortlessly, unbound.

You recall too closely
how fleeting the seduction of your madness,
how damaging your damage,
how you are addictive, then,
purged

How they resent the crash
after the delirium of you,
how quickly
men tire
of humans.

January River

You didn't say much, so I did all the talking. Chattering about my library books or the clues I'd found in the hollow of the dead tree that bridged the creek with your yard. You would wash the dishes, I would dry, and then we would have tea. Black, with a splash of citrus. I loved the flush of youth still round on your leather cheeks, and I loved the old blue and white cups we sipped from. While we waited for the water to boil, I would stand in the corridor and get lost in the Dutch still lifes, reproductions framed in dirty yellow gilt. Like the drapery in winter at the lighthouse, the paintings were heavy and distant, but I was drawn to them. They all said there was more buried in you than were gone in that winter river. I waded through the cracking paint and grime to reach for a bruised apple or a pocket watch in the fading light. I understood that the details of your silence were hidden here, among ruddy crustaceans, skinned lemons, the thin curly rind, ribbon as delicate as paper.

Elegy

Sometimes she must change continents
move
try an Italian accent with her latte
or hide behind trees

She was always somewhere,
beating drums in the Amazon
wearing necklaces of tooth and born
and late for dinner.
They would try to catch her
their nets and searchlights helpless
against the world map,
the thick and spicy incense of Africa,
the silver jangling at Mexican roadsides.

After her death,
I saw her once,
hitchhiking down a slow hot Mississippi highway.
The crimson sky stained the cotton fields bloody
on either side of that dusty ribbon.
I was weaving past scattered porches.
Someone was wailing the blues.

Ghost World

for Svetlana

"I am fated to journey hand in hand with my strange heroes and to survey the surging immensity of life..." Nikolai Gogol

The artist's house is an electric still life: a jumble of jetsam, flickering with clues to other worlds and times. She rearranges her collection like assemblage, bringing objects together for a brief encounter while furiously painting the spirit of their ensemble. You have lost track of what she is telling you because of a cupboard blooming blue and white porcelain fish and swans. You are drunk on patterns, on pen-prick constellations stabbing light through the thin rind of an Ukrainian Easter egg. There is a fireplace filled with smooth stone body parts, severed feet and hands in bloodless alabaster. A horse head book end looks on from his chess-like perch on high. His gaze shyly averts the upturned marble breasts. You are wary of the herring slabs. They are glistening pink and fatty under spare coils of onion. But their salt and slime are strangely sensual in your throat. There are, too, three-footed dishes overfilled with cashews. The artist shares a portrait of the artist as a young woman, one eye shrouded by a falling brim. She is talking about how her friend painted her just before she came to Canada. There was nothing to eat for days but a hunk of pork fat, but they had saved a bottle of goodbye champagne. Soon after, she came with her teenage daughter, and six dollars in ones, her grandmother's photo, and this canvas, rolled, cherished, on her lap, en route. It was the first work in her art collection. Now she surveys a small queendom of relics. Now she strives to tell their stories. Oil-slick beets and potatoes, on canvas, Roma scarves, a basket of dusty Soviet rubles. *Stalin was a dictator who made Hitler look like Winnie the Pooh,* your hostess blurts. Embroidery from Uzbekistan, colonized by Russia like she was. Like you were, before you were born. Watercolour landscapes by forgotten Ukraine painters, sequinned moccasins from rural Belarus. You want to crawl under the arms of the ivy on the wall, huff the heady fumes of the oily brushstrokes yet to dry. The jagged onyx clock behind the cameos is stuck at ten and twelve. Half of your DNA is tangled in all of this, but you remembered nothing before now. You were not there. Now something epigenetic is stirring, unravelling. Now you are wearing your grandmother's boots and your shovel in the frozen flesh of Saskatchewan has chipped at the clink. Strange tongues sound familiar, and the worn volumes of Gogol and Chekhov take on an aura. You will not forget again these things now marking you. You will be remade, and you do not have any say in this.

Glass

The day you shredded your hands
falling onto jagged rocks
and a broken bottle,
all I saw was the silence storming
the sky behind you,
and the silverblind light
shattering the water.
How it caught itself
on the sea-glass pale shards,
so many raw jewels
in your crucified palms.

Pretty Time Machine

"A man who views the world the same at fifty as he did at twenty has wasted thirty years of his life." Muhammad Ali

You do not have to look hard to find her: she is written on your face. Even so, you are your own, unowned, unknown, since you landed here small and perfect in the blue-brown bruise of early. You were a frail but mighty bird, unfolding, mouth mewling for her breasts. I couldn't blame you- believe me, lady, there was a time when I pined for them myself.

I will give you all of my favourite books, age appropriate, of course, saturate you in what I loved most, what I will leave behind. There will be little in the way of overlap in the books you receive from your mother, so you will have many great screeds to consider. I know that because we are old friends, and we have seldom been drawn to the same source. She has her favourite lines of poetry inked across the scars of her cutting, reclaimed territory, the body that became your body until you slipped free and fragile into our world.

Pigeon Wants a Hot Dog, Beegu, The Friendly Book: later, my scars will show, too: *Bridge to Terabithia, The Collector, The Secret History, Gentlehands.*

You will go your own way and I will not stand in your way. I am just the innocent bystander. I will follow you, I will clean up after you, I will crisscross wave my arms in warning when you approach the fire. I will not steer you clear from walking through it if that's what you insist on. Don't count on me for wisdom or clarity or the path to success- I will indulge your most dangerous, romantic illusions, I will coddle your scribbles, make Sharpie signs for your campaign: *Hello Kitty For President.*

You look just like her, and in her words, not mine, only prettier. I don't know. She's pretty pretty, then, now, clothed in this victory, even in the raw. It all becomes obvious, despite what they convinced us- the meaning of life is this, right here, you, becoming. I will accept with grace my own failures and too lates, I will accept that you are mine because she gave me that gift and you consented to it when you fell into the crook of my elbow after too many first birthday cupcakes. You are hers, so you are mine, too, in some small way, you pretty time machine.

Well, she is worried about what you will ask about her, and how she will present it, but I won't shield you with a mother's protective veil from the missteps those girls made. She was still forming, then, before all this that mattered more, finding her way, as you are, trying to poke stars and octagons through circular slots, trying to find the words.

New Orleans Jazz Bar

Sunshine shoeshine youshine moonbeam
polished snapper
jazz tapper
you, dapper, cane and coat tails
cat tails windsails

you lemon lime thing
super sweet party treat
sax blows
horn flows
trumpet crows
croons tunes of you/me
slap-slapping sweetly out to sea

Icarus, Revisited

We have landed randomly
on the subject of
airplanes, and
fear of flying.
I am not afraid, not really, I say,
I have many anxieties and
aircraft are not among them.
Mildly, he says.
He sips my latest offering,
an almost spicy
Spanish red.
Some people have had that dream,
Anthony says, some haven't.
He confesses
he has never dreamed that
he was flying. Which category are you? he
wants to know. Oh, I have,
I say, because I have,
but only the one time, and it was not
long ago. How my father loved those
dreams where he was a bird, or
a machine!
I had that peculiar brand of
little girl envy of his adventures,
he would tell me the story
and hold me on his knee.
It was strange, I tell Anthony,
I was not in any kind of

craft, I had my own wings, and I
swooped low and high,
I flew above the vineyards of
my youth, and out over
some far away ocean I don't even know.
I was spinning cotton
candy out of clouds.
The unfamiliar motion
made me seasick,
sky sickness if you will.
I felt, briefly,
a crushing wall of panic
when I became
self-conscious about
what was happening.
Even now,
with this perfect Garnacha,
I am floating
there, above an old Dutch
landscape and a
forever sea. So what did you do?
Anthony asks. I remember:
Mid-dream, I heard myself say,
remember,
you *know* you are safe in your bed,
you are asleep, and
you will land at home if
you fall. In that next moment,
there was pure, absolute liberation.
I was free of everything.
It was transcendent, I say,
because it was. And you
will have the dream, I say.

I was fortysomething
before I did. And you will have it too,
you are an imaginative,
inquisitive person and you
are going places,
you have already gone and come back
a thousand times from flight,
I see you, pacing the darkness in
pyramid shadows, looking for your lover,
you are writing, scripts
with words that break the hearts of dead men,
and you dine on maple goat cheese
and real Champagne
with ghosts whose books
you treasure.
I think about how you play your piano
after the night falls, how you fling the window
back, just a few doors down
from Glenn Gould. And from me.
And maybe that
is what I heard, those nights from across
the street burning through my sleep.
The music entered the
dark and made me dream,
how to get silver wings.

For Elaine, a Mermaid

There are claws across her face like bands
and miles and miles in her eyes.
The stars bite into her frozen hands.
She's shining in the moonlit skies.

I called her name, it sounded silver
on my slivered tongue, a gorgeous sound.
She shivered in that fiery river,
so terrified of being found.

In dreams, she is an orphan.
In daydreams, she is by the sea.
I begged for her like she was morphine,
and dreamed that she came home to me.

Feathers

Woman, you who never wore a bra, you who never guzzled wine, now have dark birds and their shrouded nest in your tit, swollen stone eggs you thought were nothing until they were something. We were at the brink of gravity when we met, our blooms long spent. Still, we were radiant with that independence of women "coming into their own." Hell's din and swell had dimmed down to a dull roar. The struggle had found formidable and seasoned foe. Well, I watched you carry the skinny drunk chick upstairs from the building backyard, holding your favourite shawl over her wet jeans on behalf of her dignity. I watched you fight like a lion for me when I made a wrong turn, and gave all my love to the wrong man. I took up your flag when a mutual friend you thought could love you, could not love you, after all. It cut us both to pieces. You boiled water until it was hissing spit, tossed tea into the cauldron, mothered my wounds with theophylline and honey. I sheltered you when her door was locked, when things turned mean. We would stake out the city from one end to the other in the caustic cold of February, or hike to Spadina to slurp spicy pork bone soup like starved and frozen explorers. And here we are, now, face to face, after everything, taking on the inevitable. It is now, or it is later, but it is what is. This wild unwinding, this unknown known. Now we await the results of scans, configure charts, see signs in winter flight, in the shrill shudder of fate and her unmoored mutterings. I can't imagine you sick or not there, beg you to stay. You tip your feathers to the wind, say, what will be, will be.

Treasures

I found an old piano
in a field of marigolds and corn
It was still haunted
by the hands that it had worn.

Forever in Blue Jeans

It's been a decade or more since I fit into my Jordaches, but your Levis are in a heap on the floor.

After, we walked, stunned, through the Fresh Co, giving careful consideration to rocket: with a squeeze of lemon, or winter tomatoes.

Crossing the icy road back to your place, we march with chins high against the falling sun, as if in a processional of sorts, with change shining and portents looming in the strange November dusk. Back inside the warm, inside you, you taste like pepper and salt and water. I brace myself against the counter, for the sting of your mouth on the back of my neck. Knife in hand, a lifetime of fences tangled in my teeth, I turn and ask for more.

Who have I become? I ask, as if you could possibly know who I have been, or who I am now. Who is this ghost of a woman, this person I am not yet quite, dicing up salad, stirring, laughing, with another human beside me, doing fake mic into an ice cream scoop to Neil Diamond on Spotify?

The cucumber, the blue glass bowl teeter perilously close to the edge.

About the Author

Lorette C. Luzajic is the founding editor of *The Ekphrastic Review*, an online journal devoted to writing inspired by art. She studied journalism at Ryerson University, but went on to pursue a more creative path writing poetry, essays, and short stories. Her work has been widely published in hundreds of local and international journals and anthologies. She has been nominated for several Best of the Net and Pushcart Prizes. Some of her poetry has been translated into Urdu. Lorette is also an award-winning visual artist whose collage paintings have been collected in more than 25 countries. Visit her at www.mixedupmedia.ca.

Publication Credits

(in order of appearance)

"The Ravine" first appeared in the author's book, *Aspartame* (Mixed Up Media Editions, 2016.)

"Violet Hill" first appeared in the author's book, *Aspartame* (Mixed Up Media Editions, 2016) and at *The Ekphrastic Review.*

"Gypsy Bisque" first appeared in the author's book, *Pretty Time Machine* (Mixed Up Media Editions, 2020) and at *MacQueen's Quinterly.*

"Crossing the River Jordan" first appeared in the author's book, *Aspartame* (Mixed Up Media Editions, 2016.)

"Gales Gas Bar" first appeared in the author's book, *The Lords of George Street,* (Mixed Up Media Editions, 2016) and at *Hood.*

"Like a Cat" first appeared in the author's book, *Solace* (Idea Fountain Books, 2011.)

"Soda" first appeared in the author's book, *Pretty Time Machine* (Mixed Up Media Editions, 2020) and at *Impspired.*

"Walking the Dark" first appeared in the author's book, *The Astronaut's Wife* (Handymaiden, 2006.)

"For JL" first appeared in the author's book, *Solace* (Idea Fountain Books, 2011.)

"Motor City Agate" first appeared in the author's book, *Pretty Time Machine* (Mixed Up Media Editions, 2020) and at *The Ekphrastic Review.*

"My Little Brother Shows Me Easter" first appeared in the author's book, *The Astronaut's Wife* (Handymaiden, 2006.)

"The Limestone Angel" first appeared in the author's book, *Pretty Time Machine* (Mixed Up Media Editions, 2020) and at *New Flash Fiction Review.*

"The Broken World" first appeared in the author's book, *The Lords of George Street,* (Mixed Up Media Editions, 2016) and at *Hood.*

"Mezcal" first appeared in the author's book, *Pretty Time Machine* (Mixed Up Media Editions, 2020) and at *Misfit Magazine.*

"In Memory" first appeared in the author's book, *The Astronaut's Wife* (Handymaiden, 2006.)

"Disappointment" first appeared in the author's book, *Pretty Time Machine* (Mixed Up Media Editions, 2020) at *Blue Heron Review,* and at *The Ekphrastic Review.*

"The Dancer" first appeared in the author's book, *Solace* (Idea Fountain Books, 2011.)

"Play Doh" first appeared in the author's book, *Pretty Time Machine* (Mixed Up Media Editions, 2020), at *Eunoia Review,* and at *Miramichi Reader.*

"Bad" first appeared in the author's book, *The Astronaut's Wife* (Handymaiden, 2006) and at *Pheobe.*

"Jean and Suzanne" first appeared in the author's book, *Solace* (Idea Fountain Books, 2011) and at *The Ekphrastic Review.*

"You Took Me Into the Woods" first appeared in the author's book, *Pretty Time Machine* (Mixed Up Media Editions, 2020) and at *Wild Word.*

"The Crayola Haikus" first appeared in the author's book, *Aspartame* (Mixed Up Media Editions, 2016.)

"Cloud Water" first appeared in the author's book, *Pretty Time Machine* (Mixed Up Media Editions, 2020) and at *L.A. Cultural Weekly.*

"Petra" first appeared in the author's book, *Aspartame* (Mixed Up Media Editions, 2016) and at *Cargo Lit.*

"Balconies" first appeared in the author's book, *Solace* (Idea Fountain Books, 2011.)

"The Sperm Trees" first appeared in the author's book, *Pretty Time Machine* (Mixed Up Media Editions, 2020), at *Eunoia Review.*

"I Am Not Afraid of Adjectives" first appeared in the author's book, *The Lords of George Street,* (Mixed Up Media Editions, 2016.)

"The Beachcomber" first appeared in the author's book, *Pretty Time Machine* (Mixed Up Media Editions, 2020) and at *L.A. Cultural Weekly.*

"The Marilyn Variations" (first appeared in the author's book, *Aspartame* (Mixed Up Media Editions, 2016) and at *The Ekphrastic Review.*

"The Piano Man" first appeared in the author's book, *Pretty Time Machine* (Mixed Up Media Editions, 2020) and at *Blue Heron Review.*

"Yakshi" first appeared in the author's book, *Aspartame* (Mixed Up Media Editions, 2016.)

"Daily Bread" first appeared in the author's book, *The Astronaut's Wife* (Handymaiden, 2006), and at *Ink* and *Tight.*

"The Photograph Not Taken" first appeared in the author's book, *The Lords of George Street,* (Mixed Up Media Editions, 2016.)

"Damage" first appeared in the author's book, *The Astronaut's Wife* (Handymaiden, 2006), and at *The People's Poet.*

"January River" first appeared in the author's book, *Pretty Time Machine* (Mixed Up Media Editions, 2020) and at *KYSO Flash.*

"Elegy" first appeared in the author's book, *The Astronaut's Wife* (Handymaiden, 2006) and at *Sidewalks, Listening Eye*, and *Other Voices.*

"Ghost World" first appeared in the author's book, *Pretty Time Machine* (Mixed Up Media Editions, 2020.)

"Glass" first appeared in the author's book, *Aspartame* (Mixed Up Media Editions, 2016.)

"Pretty Time Machine" first appeared in the author's book, *Pretty Time Machine* (Mixed Up Media Editions, 2020.)

"New Orleans Jazz Bar" first appeared in the author's book, *The Astronaut's Wife* (Handymaiden, 2006.)

"Icarus Revisited" first appeared in the author's book, *Aspartame* (Mixed Up Media Editions, 2016.)

"For Elaine, a Mermaid" first appeared in the author's book, *The Astronaut's Wife* (Handymaiden, 2006) and at *Red Coral Grotto.*

"Feathers" first appeared in the author's book, *Pretty Time Machine* (Mixed Up Media Editions, 2020) and at *Autumn Poetry Daily.*

"Treasures" first appeared in the author's book, *The Astronaut's Wife* (Handymaiden, 2006.)

"Forever in Blue Jeans" first appeared in the author's book, *Pretty Time Machine* (Mixed Up Media Editions, 2020) and in *Love Like Salt* (Love Like Salt Publishing, 2018.)

www.ingramcontent.com/pod-product-compliance
Lightning Source LLC
Chambersburg PA
CBHW060445160726
47992CB00003B/1090